To Noel &
Joann

Welcome Home
From
Grandma & Grandpa
Brian & Robert
11-8-92

# MOTHER
# & CHILD
## *in Art*

# MOTHER
# & CHILD
# *in Art*

CASSANDRA LANGER

CRESCENT BOOKS
*New York*

# Growing Up 68

# Conception & Nurturing 8

This 1992 edition was published by Crescent Books, distributed by Outlet Book Company, Inc., a Random House Company, 225 Park Avenue South, New York, New York 10003

Printed and bound in Hong Kong

ISBN 0-517-05665-8

8 7 6 5 4 3 2 1

*Mother and Child in Art* was prepared and produced by Moore & Moore Publishing, 11 W. 19th Street, New York, New York 10011

## Photo Credits

All photos courtesy of the artist or lending institution, except for the following: Black Star 121; Bridgeman/SuperStock, Inc. 34, 40, 42, 63, 64, 77; Reunion des Musées Nationaux 99; SuperStock, Inc. 30, 36–37, 60–61, 86, 94, 120.

# Contents

## The Enduring Bond 114

## Leaving the Nest 138

## AN M&M BOOK

PROJECT DIRECTOR & EDITOR  Gary Fishgall

EDITORIAL ASSISTANTS  Maxine Dormer, Ben D'Amprisi, Jr; PHOTO RESEARCH  Maxine Dormer, Janice Ostan; COPY EDITOR  Judith Rudnicki.

DESIGNER  Binns & Lubin

SEPARATIONS AND PRINTING  Regent Publishing Services Ltd.


Measurements of the paintings are in inches, height before width.

*Mother and Child In Art* invites the reader to enter into the lives of mothers and children through the ages as viewed through the eyes of a variety of artists. Drawing from a vast reservoir of world art I have attempted to gather a host of assorted and precious moments shared between mothers and children of many cultures and at various ages. The fascinating reproductions included in this volume make us aware that it is challenging to be a mother at any time anywhere in the world.

Mothers have often been given a bad shake by European culture. Our psychological theories are not kind to them. Our literature regularly terms them smothering, devouring, overprotective, and the victimizers of their children. Our films and television programs feature aloof and rejecting mothers as well as mothers who are good. Unlike other cultures which demand that children be responsible for themselves, our society demands that mothers always be there to take the blame for a child's misconduct, even when poverty, paternal abandonment, and/or other evils may have played a role in these deeds. Still, if mothers are always responsible in theory, aren't we lucky that so many of them unquestioningly accept this role in our society?

So it comes as no surprise in a culture such as ours that the child's view of the ideal mother is a woman who has no interests of her own. His or her majesty the baby's early relationship with mother has a profound effect on the sense of self and feelings about mother and about women in general.

The infant comes to define itself by internalizing the most momentous aspects of the relationship which will inform his or her understanding of the self and the world, the emotions, and the ability to love the self and others. The growing child's psychic structure and sense of reality—issues of intimacy and identification—are defined by how he or she recreates these experiences in adulthood. So the infant's actual relationship with the mother

and the feelings about her remain influential throughout life.

The artists in this book portray the human infant from its total dependence on the mother for nourishment, through its feelings of helplessness, to its need to be a separate person—learning to crawl and walk, escaping from the mother, and returning to her. They have all created works that have entered the public domain, are widely admired, timely, topical, and cross all cultural barriers. The contributors to this volume express themselves in a variety of media including pottery, sculpture, oil painting, watercolor, drawing, photography, prints, and mixed media. Clearly, as my selections illustrate, there is no medium in art that has not considered the image of the mother and child.

In general, the critical standard employed is art's usefulness to humanity in deepening our understanding of the mother and child connection. Readers will be both fascinated and delighted with the revealing glimpses that these artists give us into conception, childbirth, the drama of childhood, the companionship between mother and child, and motherly devotion. For the sake of a realistic perspective, some works that show the anxiety and difficulty in the mother-child interaction have been included as well.

By tracing these varied relationships through generations of mothers and daughters and mothers and sons, art keeps the record of motherhood alive and gives its audience invaluable insights into what it really means to be a mother or a child. *Mother and Child in Art* challenges conventional thinking regarding the theme of motherhood. It presents art with a long, rich, and rainbowed history, one which encompasses the imaginary mothers of antiquity such as the *Aztec Goddess Tlazolteotl in the Act of Childbirth*, Renaissance depictions of the Virgin and Christ child, and the abstract interpretations of our own time including works by Henry Moore and Berenice D'Vorzon. This changing parade of imagery shows that art is not a slave to its own conventions but is as diverse as the facets of mothering itself.

Above all *Mother and Child in Art* is filled with love, and its many moving images yield a wide range of stories about mothers and children that suggest what it means to be a mother or a child in all those roles'

complexities. Nor does the book shy away from difficult issues, those which are the hardest for artists to picture. A case in point is Eugene Smith's sensitive Minamata photograph of a 15-year-old quadriplegic being tenderly bathed by her mother. Another is Gabriel Metsu's *A Sick Child* in which we see a mother confronted with the near-inevitable death of her child. The many examples of women's heroism, courage, and stoicism refute any notion that they lack personal power when it comes to confronting life's realities. Through these artists' visions we are given picture after picture that affects our understanding of the intimate interaction between mother and child—their lives, family connections, and individual creative capabilities.

*Mother and Child in Art* invites the reader to witness women looking after the best interests of their children, taking care of them, raising them, and exposing them to culture or simply being supportive. It is hoped that this book will offer hours of pleasure and emotional support for the many mothers yet to be and those who are already mothers and fathers, and for the children on whom they bestow their devotion.

Finally the wealth of this record reminds us of the child that has been, the child in each of us. Looking over this record, seeing the mothers and children preserved by art's wondrous mystery, we can wholly appreciate the astonishing treasure that is childhood, here revealed in it many fascinating forms.

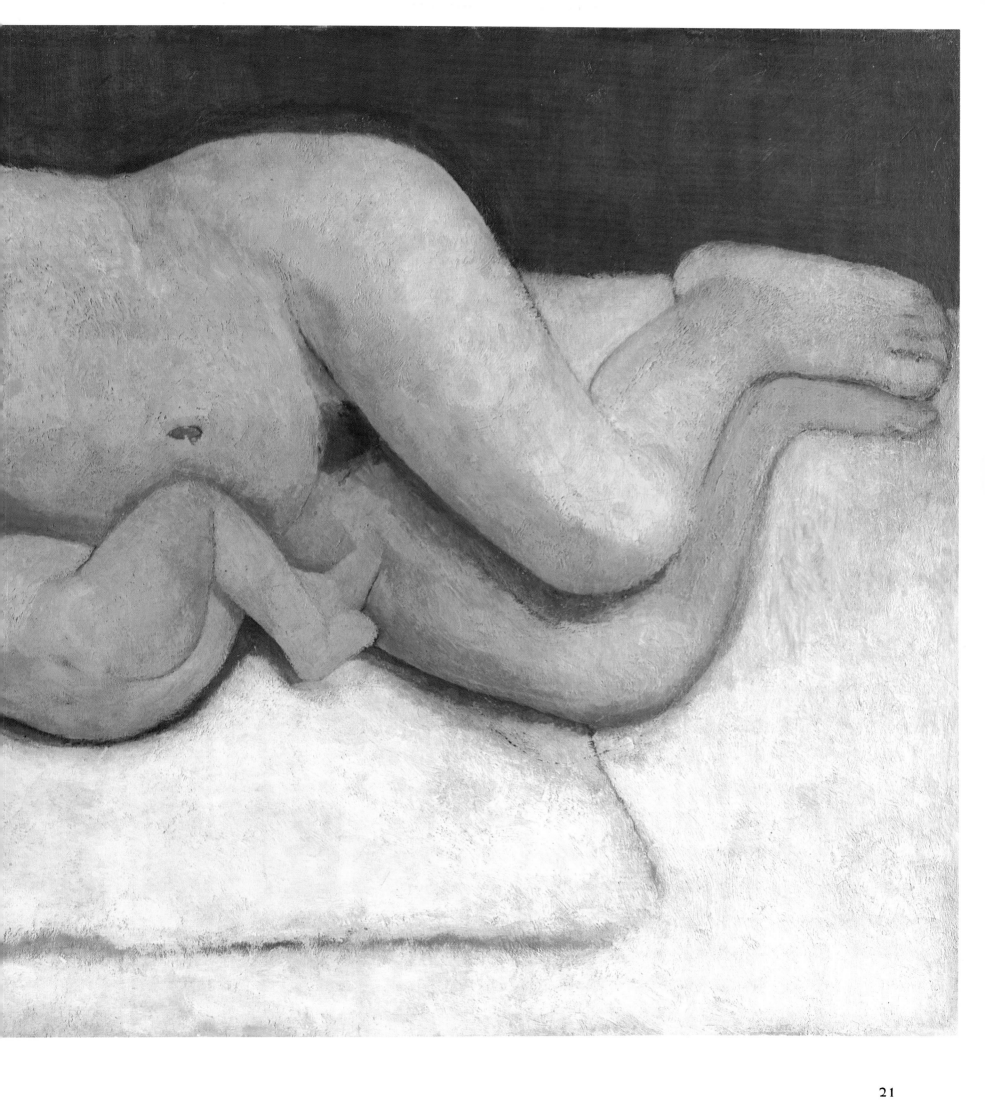

*Hospital Day, Seneca Falls, 1928*
GRACE WOODWARD, American, 1872–1967
Seneca Falls Historical Society, Seneca Falls, New York. Gelatin silver print. 9¼ x 7¹¹/₁₆ in.

## ❧ New Mothers

In Grace Woodward's day photography was considered a science rather than an art. But as an aspiring young photographer at the turn of the century, she sought to capture something of the Romanticism that characterized photography during her girlhood when photographers like Julia Margaret Cameron created highly poetic, studio-composed pictures based on Bible stories, myths, and allegories. By the time she created the present picture during the 1920s Woodward had abandoned the pictorialism and Rembrandt lighting that had first brought her public recognition, but she retained elements of her early poetic quality. And her special awareness of her sitters' individual qualities remained with her throughout her career. During her more realistic phase, her photographs often featured very strong compositions and a wicked sense of humor.

*Hospital Day, Seneca Falls* was part of a series, of which the particulars have been lost. At first it appears to be a straightforward composition of a group of unknown modern madonnas and their infants. But notice the way Woodward emphasizes in somewhat comic fashion the effect of the group spilling down the steps of the hospital like a sea of successive waves. Touches like this make her photographs more than mere records of the dress and social mores of a small town during the early part of the century. In this picture's rarified brightness, its stark and simple tonal surface, and, perhaps above all, its benign humanism, it makes a statement about American motherhood in general. Each of Woodward's handcrafted prints transcends its surface subject matter, bringing a personal concentration and beauty to issues having to do with the quality of life.

The family drama was near and dear to Eugène Carrière. In *The Young Mother*, shown at the Salon in 1879, he poured all his emotions into his subject. For him, the family was a haven that shielded the individual from the instabilities of life. Indeed, he tended to see a person's existence as one largely determined by outside factors. As he once said, "In the short span that separates birth from death, man can hardly ever make his choice of the path to be traveled." He devoted a great deal of his talent to exploring this viewpoint as it related to motherhood and childhood. In doing so, he drew upon his own memories of the maternal breast as a protection from the uncertainties and calamities of living. Thus his images depicted mother and child joined together in perfect safety, love, and trust.

He developed the picture reproduced here using his wife and infant son as the models and his own modest living quarters as the basis for the simple kitchen. While the painting is realistic, Symbolist overtones can be found in the solemn mood and religious spirit. Moreover the purity of the event—emphasized by the towel, water container, and the infant's swaddling clothes—is reminiscent of a vast body of Christian religious painting that shows the Virgin Mary and the infant Jesus in like circumstances. Despite the picture's spiritual references, its strength lies in its emotional content. By focusing on the mother nursing her child, leaving the rest of the room in semi-darkness, Carrière has created an atmosphere of genuine affection and tenderness. In this picture he depicts the moods, thoughts, and inner life—as well as the beauty—of motherhood.

*The Young Mother,* 1879
EUGÈNE CARRIÈRE, French, 1849–1909
Avignon, Musée Calvet, France. Oil on canvas.
58 x 45¾ in.

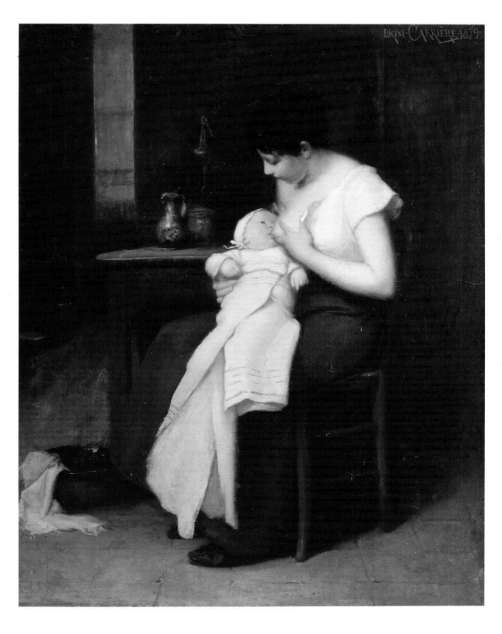

*A Lady Having Her Hair Dressed While She Nurses Her Child, 12th Dynasty*
EGYPTIAN (Middle Kingdom), 2000–1788 B.C.
The Metropolitan Museum of Art, New York City, Rogers Fund, 1922. Stone. Height 2¾ in.

## ≈ Bliss

*Nursing Mother Having her Hair Dressed* was created during a period referred to as the Middle Kingdom. It was a time when Egypt was reunified and the central monarchy was reestablished. During this interval the Egyptians developed a mythology that personified and deified nature and her powers. How did the statue shown here reflect the mythology?

Ancient peoples considered the center to be the most sacred element of something—be it an object, a person, or a space. Its center was its core, the site of creative being, the Most Holy. An extension of this thinking viewed the mother as the center of the universe because she created life—it grew, or so they believed, in the form of the embryo from her navel. The soft, flowing contours of the sculpture reproduced here represent the mystical transformation of a woman's body during pregnancy and mirror the primal feelings shared between the life-giver and her newborn.

In this delightful carving, the mother, who is part of the Egyptian court, devotes her attention to the baby in her lap leaving her servant to arrange her hair into one of the highly stylized patterns that were popular during this era. For the baby, this is a time of deep attachment to its mother's body. It is a period—particularly during feeding—when all sorts of meanings flow between parent and child. As the child grows, he or she will increasingly seek to establish a clear differentiation between itself and its mother. Parent and child will never be quite so intimately linked again.

The Egyptian artist who made this work understood the silent, poetic language that passes between a mother and her child when suckling. Drawing on the rhythms and forces that bond the two individuals, he creates an attractively informal interpretation of maternity, one that served to influence the course of Western art.

Anique Taylor, artist, poet, and professional clown, also has a keen understanding of babyhood. In this sensitive drawing, she reveals what psychologists are just beginning to discover, that every infant is endowed with incredible sensibilities. At as early as three weeks of age, for example, a baby can discriminate between his or her mother and other faces and voices. Moreover, an infant's visual motor system is virtually mature. Thus, he or she can use that potent form of communication—gazing—just as adults do.

The close relationship between mother and child is often enhanced through breastfeeding. For many a woman this form of nurturing is fundamental to the all-encompassing relationship that she develops with her newborn during the latter's first few weeks of life. During this period, a new mother typically gives herself up and becomes one with her baby as she discovers the wonder of a brand new being who is at once part her own self and yet separate from and outside of her.

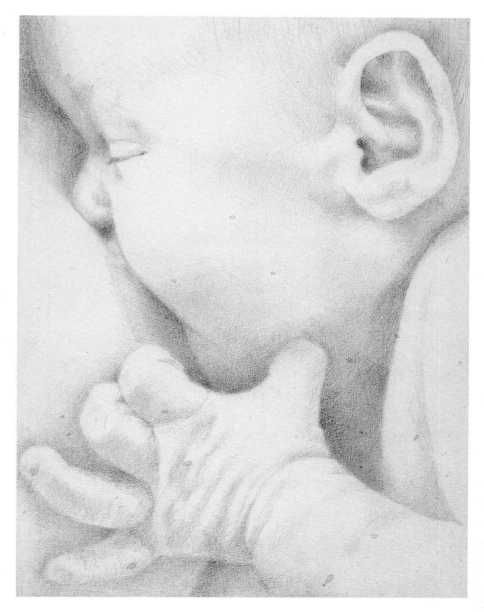

*Mother and Child,* 1989
ANIQUE TAYLOR, American
Courtesy of the artist, New York City. Graphite on paper.
4½ x 6 in.

In *Mother and Child,* the relationship of the newborn to the mother is shown as crucial to the baby's psychological and physical development. The infant relates solely to the mother, in reality and fantasy; the attachment is almost addictive. By placing her emphasis on the feeding baby, the artist revels in the infant's fantasy—that he or she can fullfill his or her desire at any given moment. And how wonderful it is when the infant's desire is to be fed and the mother magically offers her breast at precisely the right time.

**B**orn in Beijing, China, Madame Jin Gao began studying painting at the Central Fine Arts Academy in 1948, one year before the People's Republic of China was founded. After the usual five-year program was condensed, she graduated in 1952, ready to serve the revolution as an artist. She was particularly drawn to the Impressionist paintings of the 19th-century French artists Claude Monet, Paul Cézanne, and Camille Pissarro.

At the time of her graduation, the newly "liberated" nation was in need of artists willing to work in rural areas. Jin Gao chose an assignment in Huhehot City, Inner Mongolia, where she served as the editor of *Hua Bao*, China's art magazine. There she began to explore the theme that has preoccupied her for more than 30 years—that of mother and child—which she believes to be at the heart of civilization. As she captures the spirit and customs of the place she calls home, she uses a combination of Western painting techniques and Oriental design elements.

*The Woodland Cradle*, seen here, seems like an illustration from a Mongolian fairy tale. It depicts a young mother who has stolen a moment from picking gooseberries to play with her infant, whose cradle is fastened to the branch of a nearby tree. Mongolian women are a prominent theme in Madame Jin's work. The beauty that she sees in their lives is expressed through an essentially Impressionist palette with a one-color accent that—to use a musical metaphor—sets the melody for her picture. It is an unusual but effective approach, one that enables her to convey visually emotions that are otherwise intangible. The spectrum of creativity encompassed by her realism reveals itself in paintings that revitalize tradition and have a contemporary, yet universal significance.

*The Woodland Cradle*, 1985
**MADAME JIN GAO**, Chinese
Grand Central Art Galleries, New York City. Oil on canvas.
56¾ x 35⅞ in.

The art of the Netherlands reached its apogee in the work of Rembrandt, the most imaginative and versatile Dutch painter of all time. His passionate observations on human nature imbued his paintings with a deep compassion, and his decisive use of light and shadow—seemingly bound up in some mysterious way with his spiritual life—was brilliantly original. He first achieved success as a portrait painter and later transformed the stories of the Old Testament into living pictures.

In *The Holy Family* Rembrandt shows the Virgin Mary tenderly hovering over the sleeping Jesus' cradle. Joseph, Mary's husband, can be seen at the far left working by the light of the window. Near him is an elderly woman tenderly adjusting the child's wrappings in typical grandmotherly fashion. She is unidentified but her presence humanizes the scene in the fashion of 17-century Dutch narratives.

In this work, Rembrandt transforms Joseph's stark, humble carpentry shop, with its cluttered interior, into a space suggesting the power of unseen things. It is as though God Himself is present in the indirect light that is cast over Mary and the sleeping Savior. Shades of sienna illumination separate the bright and dark colors, mysteriously intensifying the restrained harmonies of the canvas.

This is a riveting painting, with its velvety shimmer of glowing lights, strong sense of composition, tender emotional power, and singed mahogany background heightened by specks of sparkling red. The picture expresses an intense devotional poetry usually reserved for nativity scenes.

*The Holy Family, 1640*
REMBRANDT HARMENSZ VAN RIJN, Dutch, 1606–1669
The Louvre, Paris. Oil on panel. 16¼ x 13¼ in.

FOLLOWING PAGES: DETAIL
*The Holy Family*

## ✣ *Two Mothers, Four Mothers*

Sir Edwin Landseer loved to portray the noble and human qualities of animals, most especially dogs. In the work reproduced here, *A Highland Breakfast*, he does so and at the same time gives viewers a slice of rural life in the Scottish highlands. Particularly notable is the juxtaposition of human and canine behavior with a Highland mother breastfeeding her baby while the dogs eat their breakfast. One of the terriers suckles her puppies mirroring the human mother's ministrations. On the far side of the food tub a third terrier looks on as a deerhound and a collie dispute over a bone.

In this meticulously rendered interior, the brown and gold shadows cast a tender light on the figures. The two light sources, the window at left and the chimney opening at right, throw the rugged stone hearth into sharp relief while casting highlights on the wooden crib, the tub, the woman's white cap, and the earthenware bowl containing the woman's breakfast. Touches of

red on the baby's cap and the blanket in the crib add interest and freshness to the composition.

Seen in profile at left the mother is a simply dressed, unpretentious, pretty young woman who tenderly nurses her baby. The dogs at right with their contrasting coats and colors serve to accentuate the rich surface textures of the painting and to underscore the strong characters of those who inhabit this rustic environment. The atmosphere is peaceful and heartwarming, conveying the homey domestic values of the typical Highland family.

In the boldly colorful painting on page 31, Charleen Touchette draws upon her French-Canadian and Native American heritage to represent the mothers of the world united with their children and each other in peace and love. The picture is part of a series of paintings inspired by a vision that the artist experienced in 1983. In her vision, Touchette saw what she calls the Four Colors of People—Red, Yellow, Black, and White—sitting around the Tree of Life nursing their babies in harmony. From this experience, she came to realize

that though different people enjoy different customs, beliefs, and modes of behavior and that each takes pride in its own culture, all of humankind shares a common connection by virtue of its way of birthing and nurturing life and by its concern for future generations. "Our experiences as daughters, sisters, mothers, and grandmothers," Touchette says, "can provide a common bond that transcends our differences."

*We Are The Same But We Are Different* shows four women—an Asian, a European, an African, and a Native American—nursing their babies of different ages in the shade of the Tree of Life, which stands beneath the Sacred Mountain with the River of Life flowing around it. Touchette's model for this circle is the Indian Medicine Wheel which includes every shade of human being in the world and features at the four key intersections the Four Colors of People. According to Indian belief, there is an interrelated order to everything in the universe and everyone in the circle must contribute equally to the whole in order for harmony to be achieved. Native Americans also maintain that the human psyche needs art which they and Touchette believe is drawn from divine inspiration, visions, and dreams. Art from such sources is expected to inspire people to turn the symbols of reality—art—into behavior in everyday life.

In keeping with the traditions of Touchette's people, the symbols in her work are used to foster the higher goals of all humankind. She believes that "respect, honesty, and the willingness to express our feelings and to forgive and accept each other can make it work." In her compositions one finds the artist's active spiritual desire to transform the material world and to connect with what she calls "The Breath of Life," which is humankind's spiritual consciousness of all things.

*A Highland Breakfast*, 1834
SIR EDWIN HENRY LANDSEER, English, 1802–1873
Victoria and Albert Museum, London. Oil on canvas.
20 x 26 in.

*We Are The Same But We Are Different*, c.1987
CHARLEEN TOUCHETTE, Canadian
Courtesy of the artist. Mixed media on paper. 30 x 22 in.

FOLLOWING PAGES: DETAIL
*A Highland Breakfast*

*Madonna and Child
on a Curved Throne,
late 13th century*
BYZANTINE

National Gallery of Art,
Washington, D. C.,
Andrew W. Mellon Collection.
Tempera on panel.
32⅛ x 19⅜ in.

## ❧ Madonna and Child

During the pre-Renaissance period an artist's skills were tightly harnessed to the service of the Church, as altarpieces, wall-paintings (frescoes), decorative panels, and shrines became the primary outlets for his work. The work reproduced here stands as a testament to the tenacity of the workshop system that was at the heart of the art of the Middle Ages. The Madonna and Christ child are painted in a thin film on a highly reflective gold surface that forms the highlights, halos, and the background so that even the shadows never seem wholly opaque. In addition, the gold foil in the background serves to fill the picture with light, giving it something of the quality of a stained-glass window.

This Madonna Enthroned is one of the earliest proto-Renaissance attempts to humanize the depiction of the Virgin. The previous traditions of Byzantine art tended to emphasize Mary's connection with the spiritual world, showing her as a marionette-like figure seated on a throne that usually reflected a marked interest in architectural patterning. The painter of the *Madonna and Child on a Curved Throne*, by contrast, roots Mary in the real world, articulating a relationship between her and Jesus that calls to mind the interaction that takes place between ordinary mothers and children. What this picture does is posit a relationship between earthly and heavenly unions of mother and child which flowered into the creative unity of portrayals of Madonna and Child in the High Renaissance.

During his later years, Paul Gauguin, the great mystic of Post-Impressionism, escaped from European civilization and fled to Polynesia where he created some of the most evocative paintings in the history of modern art. Forceful in the expression of his ideas, Gauguin believed that art was something one envisioned through dreams and the contemplation of nature before the act of creation. He painted from memory, his imagination freely translating his experiences into spiritual visions.

The title of the painting reproduced here translates as "I hail thee, Mary," which were the archangel's first words to the Virgin when he told her that she would bear the Son of God. The figure of Gabriel, distinguished primarily by his golden wings, can barely be seen at left in the picture. Opposite him at right (as was customary in Renaissance versions of the Annunciation) is a Polynesian Virgin Mary, a halo around her head and the infant Christ child on her shoulder. Her lithe form is counterbalanced by the heaviness of the child as he rests against her. Two other young women bow in supplication.

In *Orana Maria*, as in many of Gauguin's Tahitian paintings, the artist attempts to reconcile art and nature, as well as religion and the spiritual, by creating a new Eden. Using bold orange, brilliant blue, and Veronese green, he conjures up an enchanted, tropical land, luxuriant and primitive, whose inhabitants are modest and unspoiled. Through the simplification of color, shape, and texture, he forges rhythmic and geometric relationships between the young women who populate the canvas and their lush surroundings. The result is a composition carefully arranged primarily as a means of rehabilitating Christian mythology through a return to the primitive. It expresses at the same time an enviable harmony between the natural world and its human inhabitants.

*continued*

*Orana Maria,*
*c. 1891—1893*
PAUL GAUGUIN, French,,
1848–1903
The Metropolitan Museum of Art,
New York City,
Bequest of Sam A. Lewisohn, 1951.
Oil on canvas. 44¾ x 34½ in.

FOLLOWING PAGES: DETAIL
*Orana Maria*

Called the prince of painters, Raphael has been universally acknowledged as an artist of genius. Critics have praised him for the purity of his designs, the nobility of his ideas, the beauty of his facial types, the elegance of his forms and drapery, and the brilliance of his compositional groupings. By consulting the works of ancient sculptors, he learned how to select details that could be incorporated into his own compositions. He painted only the most essential, beautiful, and perfect of forms, which to him meant those with a regularity of proportion, a luminosity of color, and a smoothness of finish. The gentleness of Raphael's own nature is reflected in the humanity with which he imbued his paintings of mothers and children.

Raphael's conceptions of beauty are admirably reflected in this depiction of a blonde Virgin in a red robe. On her lap is the infant Jesus, his hand casually grasping his mother's bodice as he looks out at the viewer. The golden-fleshed Mary is seen full front, her body at a slight angle and her perfectly contoured oval face set against a soft, pastoral backdrop with a lake in the far left and a church atop a hill at right.

Raphael's emphasis on the swaying rhythm of the tall trees, the flowing sensuality of the field, and the arcadian mood that unifies the entire canvas reveals the artist's debt to the poetic model furnished by the Roman writer Virgil, who inspired many other Renaissance artists as well. Raphael's vision of the Virgin and Jesus and their perfect harmony with nature suggests something of the undeniable bond that all mothers share with Mother Nature. His interpretation of the mother-and-child theme, like that of the 19th-century English painter Edward Burne-Jones, reflects a deliberate reworking of an older pagan tradition in order to make it conform to the conventions of Christianity.

*The Small-Cowper Madonna,* c.1505
RAPHAEL, Italian, 1483–1520
National Gallery of Art, Washington, D.C.,
Widener Collection. Oil on panel. 23⅜ x 17⅜ in.

DETAIL
*The Small-Cowper Madonna*

## ❧ Out of Doors

Agnes M. Richmond moved to New York in 1888 to study at the Art Students League. By the turn of the century she had achieved a reputation as a portraitist and had won numerous prizes for her work. From 1910 to 1914 she taught at the League. The bulk of her work consisted of portraits of women who came from a variety of social backgrounds.

The depiction of the young mother in this picture was strongly influenced by the work of the American Impressionist Mary Cassatt, by Japanese woodblock prints, and by J. A. M. Whistler, who espoused the notion of "art for art's sake." The two figures are seen in an outdoor setting which allowed Richmond to experiment with the principles of *plein-air* painting developed by the French Impressionist master Claude Monet.

Richmond vividly conveys the personalities of her models and their relationship. The mother is seen in profile, facing right and wearing a pale aqua-and-salmon kimono with darker spirals and the image of a sacred mountain set against a faint stencil of tree branches patterned upon it. She gazes past the infant that she holds close to her body as if lost in some private revery. The blonde child, dressed in shimmering white, looks directly at the viewer, her tiny left hand resting confidently on her mother's arm. Richmond's controlled, realistic depiction of mother and child is contrasted with the general harmony of the sumptuous chrome-yellow-and-celadon green background and the artist's dashing brushwork.

Largely self-taught, John Edward Costigan developed a highly individual way of painting directly from nature. He began his career as a palette-knife artist, but he quickly changed over to brushes which he typically loaded with generous helpings of paint. Placing short dabs of broken color on the canvas, he created a vibrating effect similar to that achieved by the French Impressionists.

*Mother and Child, c. 1905*
AGNES MILLEN RICHMOND, American, 1870–1964
Grand Central Art Galleries, New York City. Oil on canvas. 30 x 24 in.

While living in New York City, Costigan, like most artists, explored the many local galleries and museums, but in 1910 he moved to Orangeburg, New York, where he lived contentedly on his own wooded acres. Thereafter, he became an eminently successful painter of rural life. His highly textured, impastoed surfaces have a unity of subject matter that is rooted in America's agrarian past.

In *Woman, Child and Goat* Costigan enhances nature's transformative powers by using a palette of vivid autumn reds, browns, saffrons, and lush springtime greens against a dazzling white background. The focus here is on a woman wearing a white blouse and a long reddish skirt who tends her baby and her flock in the woods. The figures of the mother and the child are lovingly described, showing the artist's deep respect for the maternal spirit.

Reflecting the artist's own feelings about nature, this painting presents a view of childhood that is in harmony with the natural world and its creatures and a view of motherhood that is joyous and serene. As such it is part of a genre of pastoral paintings with an enormously rich symbolic tradition behind it.

*Woman, Child and Goat, c. 1925*
JOHN EDWARD COSTIGAN, American, 1888–1972
Grand Central Art Galleries, New York City. Oil on canvas 45 x 45 in.

FOLLOWING PAGES: DETAIL
*Woman, Child and Goat*

By the end of the 1930s Philip Guston had developed an abstract style that departed sharply from the social realism of his earlier years. For a time he oscillated between the two conflicting styles. *The Young Mother*, painted in 1944, is a product of this period.

In the fall of 1941 when he was 28 years old, Guston went to the University of Iowa to teach. He remained there for four years during which he created this portrait of his wife Musa and their daughter Musette set against a view from his studio window which shows St. Mary's Church on the right. The painting alludes to the various styles that Guston was hoping to reconcile during this stage of his career. He wanted to unite the geometry and light of the Renaissance master Piero della Francesca with the slightly abstract

### The Young Mother, 1944

PHILIP GUSTON, Canadian-American, 1913–1980

The University of Iowa Museum of Art, Iowa City, Gift of Dr. Clarence Van Epps. Oil on canvas. 39⁷/₁₆ x 29½ in. Photo by C. Randall Tosh.

but still classical art of such 20th-century masters as Giorgio de Chirico, Pablo Picasso, Georges Braque, and Fernand Léger.

In deference to Piero, *The Young Mother* reflects Renaissance prototypes, particularly paintings of the Madonna and Christ child. But it also mirrors the regionalism of the artist's friend Grant Wood. Even though Guston was more interested in the School of Paris than he was in Wood's midwestern brand of realism, *The Young Mother* derives from both traditional figurative styles and a more surreal modernism. Consider, for example, such features as the slightly smiling, blue cat in the background on the table to the right of the mother, the cubistic flattening of the various planes found in the child's white jacket, the chair, the green building set in shallow space against the tree, and the clear blue sky. All of these elements reveal Guston's assimilation of the Cubist principles of Picasso and Braque. The child's blue toy cat with its odd shape and perpetually popping eyes is

a cartoonlike character who mirrors Guston's own sardonic reflections on the Walt Disney world of postwar America.

During the late 1940s Pablo Picasso turned his attention toward the theme of mother and child with a fresh sense of excitement. The composition shown here, considered by Alfred Barr, director of New York's Museum of Modern Art from 1929–1943, to be one of the artist's finest wartime canvases, reflects Picasso's understanding of the deep emotional bond that exists between a mother and her child and how that bond nurtures a toddler as he or she leaves infancy and enters the world of childhood. Through his drawing, composition, color, and magnified scale, Picasso suggests the momentous drama of the scene, not its charm.

The painting depicts Picasso's maid Inez and her toddler son who is learning to walk alone. Taking those first steps represents a critical moment in any youngster's life for as he or she does so, he or she moves from the neonatal state of symbiosis with the mother to the articulation of an individual posture in life, one which will eventually lead to independent status. The child here is well beyond lifesize so that his awkwardly raised foot, his face screwed tight with effort, and the overarching figure of the mother take on a somewhat monumental character.

From an adult perspective, the sight of a child starting to propel himself or herself into space is both funny and touching, but for the child it is a moment full of danger in which eagerness, determination, and insecurity are mingled with triumph. It is an affirmation of self and the beginning of a healthy separation from the mother. This moment is significant for the child's maternal protector too because it signals the time when she can relax a bit, when she can let go of the responsibilities that come with nurturing an infant and begin to enjoy watching the young child progress toward maturity.

### First Steps, 1943

PABLO PICASSO, Spanish, 1881–1973

Yale University Art Gallery, New Haven, Connecticut, Gift of Stephen C. Clark, B.A. 1903. Oil on canvas. 51¼ x 38¼ in.

Nurtured by the Nile River, Egyptian civilization looked upon mothering as a central component of society and religion. Fertility was highly prized and mothers and children formed the domestic core of a sex-gender system in which parenting was assumed to be a woman's primary responsibility.

This small sculpture from the Old Kingdom shows a seated mother suckling an infant while a toddler clings to her elbow. The child's gesture shows that she embraces what she loves. Indeed, this seems to be a happy family unit all around. The woman obviously enjoys her relationship with her breastfed baby yet, at the same time, she continues to provide warmth and comfort to her older child. Her affection and devotion are openly and honestly portrayed by the unknown sculptor.

This work reveals the sophistication of Egyptian artisans who had perfected their skills in a limited field of endeavor. The maker adhered well to established compositional conventions, including the use of lavish patterning in the waves of hair and a high degree of naturalism in the domestic details. The diminutive scale, refined carving, and fine limestone reveal the hand of a highly skilled craftsman who was able to endow this work with a sense of monumentality despite the small size of its figures.

Egon Schiele was part of the avant-garde art movement in Vienna, Munich, and other European cities during the early years of the 20th century. In 1907, while he was still a student at the Vienna Academy of Fine Arts, he met Gustav Klimt, a major figure in Viennese art, whose work had inspired Schiele to become part of the modernist vanguard. He had his first comprehensive one-man show at the Hans Glotz Gallery in Munich in 1913. By 1915, he had been drafted into the Austrian army but he continued painting. The immediate results of Schiele's World War I period can be seen in his *Mother and Two Children*, with its flat decorative patterning, elongated figures, stylized forms, and jewel-like color.

By the time he painted this work Schiele had begun to concentrate primarily on the human figure. Based on his earlier mother and child allegories, this picture consists of sharp, nervous contours which he filled in with thin washes of color. His figures are shown in deliberately inelegant poses, their forms unidealized and highly distorted. The woman's head, for example, is wrapped in a white shroud that makes her pale, attenuated face look like a death mask. The three angular figures are linked together by a white blanket spread across the mother's lap. The overlapping folds of the golden comforter, with a houndstooth pattern, wrap around their feet and entwine with the fringes of the red blankets.

The artist used the figure of the infant Toni, his nephew, twice in the same picture. The children are constructed like two puppets or dolls on display in a department store. They are richly dressed in a highly colorful patchwork of green, red, yellow, and brown. The children symbolize a variety of dual characteristics—the extroverted and the introverted, the religious and the worldly, the passive and the active, perhaps even life and death. When he couldn't get Toni to pose, Schiele sometimes used a small Japanese doll that he kept in his studio, which may account for the wooden aspects of the figures in this picture.

*Mother and Two Children,*
*5th-6th Dynasty*
EGYPTIAN (Old Kingdom),
2345–2181 B.C.
The Metropolitan Museum of Art,
New York City,
Gift of Edward S. Harkness , 1926.
Painted limestone. Height 4¾ in.

*Mother and Two Children*, 1915–1917
EGON SCHIELE, Austrian, 1890–1918
Österreichisches Museum für Angewandte Kunst, Vienna. Oil on canvas. 59 x 62½ in.

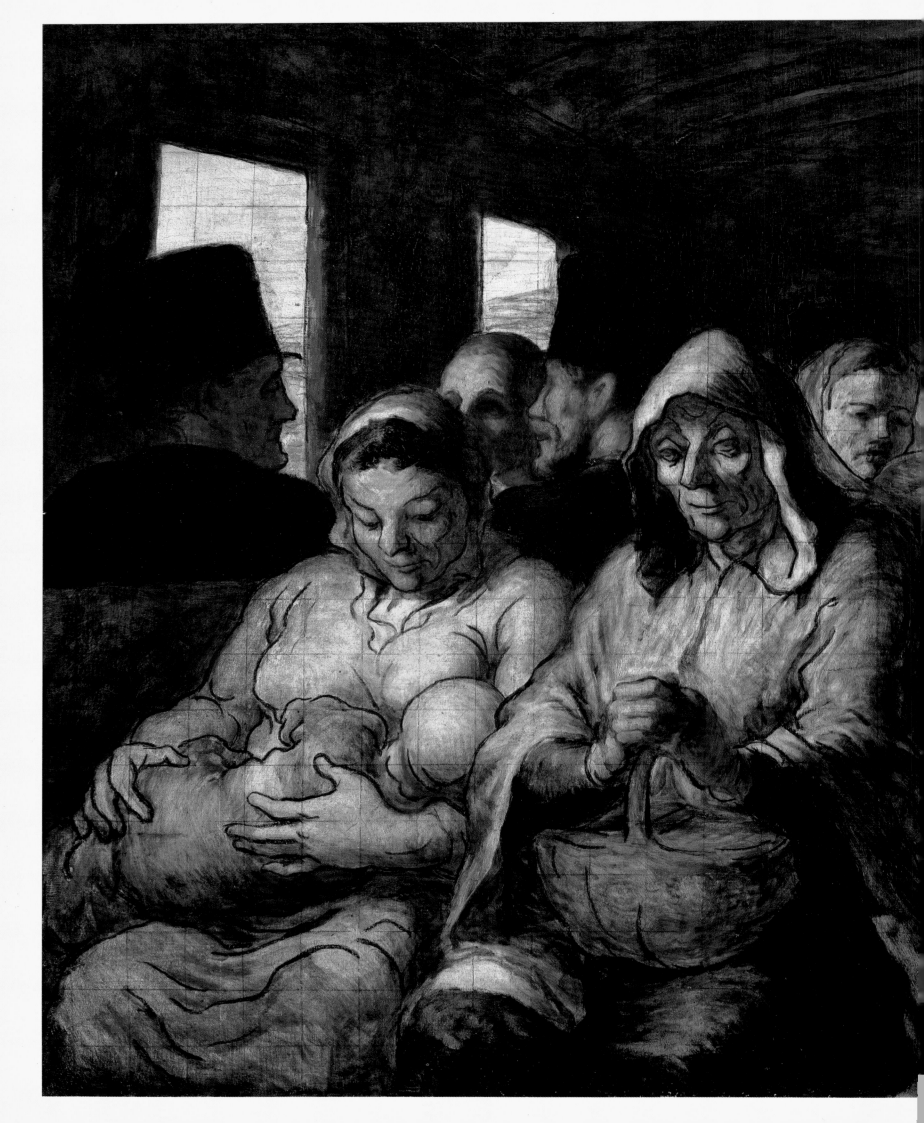

Honoré Daumier was a great Romantic artist working in the graphic and social traditions of the Spanish painter Francisco José de Goya y Lucientes. Because Daumier did not shrink from depicting the material conditions of the lower classes and the urban realities of his day—not typical subjects for high art in 19th-century France, or anywhere else for that matter—he remained practically unknown as a painter during his lifetime, although he was renowned for his satirical cartoons and caricatures. Nonetheless, his paintings were significant for their honest portrayals of the changes in lifestyles and living conditions brought on by industrialization. His subjects, especially the poor, were endowed with a monumentality and a nobility of which they were often robbed in daily life. His famous painting *Third Class Carriage* exemplifies the artist's respect for the dignity of human life. Painted very freely, it has a raw power that derives from Daumier's own passionate commitment to an ideal and humane social order.

In this picture the artist's sympathetic portrayal of working-class people encompasses various age groups who have nothing in common with one another except for the fact that they are all traveling in an uncomfortable third-class railway car. Although they are physically crowded together, patiently enduring the discomforts of class-discriminatory public transportation, they take no notice of each other.

*continued*

*Third Class Carriage*, c. 1863–1865
HONORÉ DAUMIER, French, 1808–1879
The Metropolitan Museum of Art, New York City, Bequest of Mrs. H.O. Havemeyer, 1929, The H.O. Havemeyer Collection, Photo by Malcolm Varon. Oil on canvas. 25¾ x 35½ in. Photo by Malcolm Varon.

The central focus of the composition is the mother and infant who are locked in a close embrace as the baby draws nourishment from the woman's breast. Next to her sits a serene old woman who may be the baby's grandmother. This majestic matriarch holds a basket of food on her lap. Perhaps it symbolizes humanity's enduring hope for a social transformation that will transcend the oppressive features of human existence. Beside the woman sleeps a young boy, perhaps the elder child of the nursing mother.

Marisol Escobar is a self-taught sculptor whose work is strongly influenced by American folk art and Pre-Columbian pottery. A subject of major interest to her throughout her career has been the family. Many of her works in this vein have exposed the stereotype of the happy wife and mother. Indeed, motherhood in particular has been sharply targeted in her art.

During the 1960s, Marisol dealt several times with the mother-child theme, using anonymous types who bear her own features. Her mother died when she was 11 years old and the sculptures from this period express her feelings about her personal loss. The piece shown here, created in 1962, is indicative of her unique style, which uses interlocking shapes of flat color with clearly defined edges.

In *The Family* she plays with the tension between the members of a nuclear family while, at the same time, examining the strong emotional connotations attached to the age-old mother-child relationship. This sculpture is based on a cast-off photograph that the artist found among some wastepaper near her studio. The names and histories of the models are unknown. But through the use of exaggeration, the impassive faces of the figures, and the boxes or containers that hold the work together while hiding the subjects' bodies, Marisol teases viewers in a highly sophisticated and playful way, inviting speculation on the lives of these people. How interesting are they behind the masks they wear, one might wonder.

The artist's sense of design unifies the disparate elements in her compositions so that the realities she juggles become powerful and surreal. Despite her own reservations concerning the state of Western culture, she presents this mother and her children as identifiable symbols of strength and courage. They are separate individuals yet united by family ties.

*The Family,* 1962
MARISOL ESCOBAR, American, 1930–
The Museum of Modern Art, New York City,
Advisory Commitee Fund.
Painted, carved wood. Height 6 ft. 10⅝ in.

## ♣ Celebrating

Katsukawa Shunshō's reputation stems primarily from his striking prints of Japan's *kabuki* theater, but he also produced a number of works featuring beautiful women. Among these stunning prints, in which he depicted the feminine manners and morals of his day, are several on the subject of motherhood. One of these, *Celebrating Boy's Day*, is seen here.

Boy's Day is one of Japan's favorite holidays since it celebrates the birth of the young male children who bring new life to the society and mark the continuation of the family line. The subject provided Shunshō with an ideal opportunity to indulge his taste for intricate patterning and great diversity of colors.

In this woodblock print from the classic period of *ukiyo-e*, the artist endows his mother and child with the voluptuous, technically skillful sensuality and refined sweetness that became his hallmark as a portraitist of beautiful women. Taking as his theme the day-to-day relationship of mother and child, he shows a group of women and a boy dressed in red, the traditional color of good luck. In concentrating on the relationship between the lusty, mischievous lad and his mother, Shunshō portrays the deep, elemental involvement that they share and their intense emotional feelings for one another. At the same time, he seems to recognize that a gradual transition will occur in their relationship as they move from a uniquely shared interconnection to individuation.

*Celebrating Boy's Day*, c. 1780
KATSUKAWA SHUNSHŌ, Japanese, 1726–1792
Museum of Art, Carnegie Institute, Pittsburgh, Bequest of
Dr. James B. Austin. Woodblock. 15⅜ x 10 in.

DETAIL
*Celebrating Boy's Day*

## ♣ Mother with Boy and Girl

Few men have reached the heights in art and diplomacy attained by Peter Paul Rubens. Because of his courtly manners and linguistic skills he was entrusted by Maria de' Medici, the Queen consort of Henry IV of France, with one of the crowning achievements of his career, a series of large-scale paintings covering her life for the Palais du Luxembourg in Paris (the series is now in the Louvre). He was also knighted by both Philip IV of Spain and Charles I of England who greatly appreciated his technical virtuosity and aristocratic style. Particularly admired was the coloristic vitality of his work, for which Rubens was indebted to the Venetian master Titian. Acknowledging Titian's influence, he once said that he was "as in love with Titian as a bridegroom with his bride."

In 1630 Rubens, then 53 years old and a widower, married Hélène Fourment, a girl of 16, who was to bear him five children. In the work reproduced here, *Helena Fourment, 2nd Wife of Peter Paul Rubens and Their Two Children,* he depicts his second wife and two of their youngsters. There is something exquisitely skillful in the coloring of the flesh, which is opulent and glowing, and the composition, which is complex, expansive, and vigorous. Hélène is a figure of great charm and gaiety, the perfect embodiment of beautiful motherhood. Rubens shows her playing with the children as they sit for their portrait. The little boy demands a great deal of attention

while his sister appears preoccupied. Hélène seems to take a great deal of pride in her offspring, especially the little boy. Or perhaps this is a reflection of Rubens' own reaction to his new family. Either way the artist was at the full height of his powers when he painted this canvas. It is one of the most lyrically beautiful pictures that his skilled hand ever created.

Mme. Charpentier's salons were celebrated. Everyone of note in the French literary, art, and political worlds attended her famous Friday gatherings. At these affairs Renoir became acquainted

*continued*

DETAIL
*Helena Fourment, 2nd Wife of Peter Paul Rubens and Their Two Children*

*Helena Fourment, 2nd Wife of Peter Paul Rubens and Their Two Children,* c.1636
PETER PAUL RUBENS, Flemish, 1577–1640
The Louvre, Paris. Oil on panel. 44½ x 32¼ in.

with the most influential people of his day. He also came to know the Charpentier family well.

The portrait of Mme. Charpentier and her children was painted in 1878. It is set in the family's small, so-called Japanese salon. Mme. Charpentier is attired in a long black dress by celebrated fashion designer Charles Worth which in itself presented a challenge for the artist to render. She is placed center stage on a sofa, beaming proudly at her children. Seated next to her is her son Paul and perched comfortably on a large, benign dog is her daughter Georgette. In this work Renoir projects a positive view of parent-child ties. Indeed, Mme. Charpentier and her children seem independent of mind, full of vigor, and content to focus their attention on their own thoughts and activities. The flowing Worth dress and the children's simple costumes—the boy dressed identically to the girl—reflect the down-to-earth informality that characterized this household.

*Madame Charpentier and Her Children* enjoyed great success at the 1879 Salon. Perhaps it was because, as Renoir explained, "Madame Charpentier reminded me of my early loves: the women Fragonard painted."

The writer Marcel Proust was particularly impressed by Renoir's ability to depict "the poetry of an elegant home and the exquisite gowns of our time." As a result of this commission, the 37-year-old artist was hailed as a great figure painter.

*Madame Charpentier and Her Children,*
*1878*
PIERRE AUGUSTE RENOIR, French, 1841–1919
The Metropolitan Museum of Art, New York City,
Wolfe Fund, 1907. Catherine Lorillard Wolfe Collection.
Oil on canvas. 60½ x 74⅞ in.

# ♣ Comfort

The French Impressionists had a revolutionary effect on the development of painting throughout Europe and the United States during the latter part of the 19th century and the first quarter of the 20th century. They saw color in the natural world as fragmented particles of light which they replicated in art by applying broken dabs of various colors next to each other, leaving the eye of the viewer to mix the colors optically as he or she studied the canvas. Instead of the nearly invisible brush strokes of the French Academic artists of the day, the Impressionists left all sorts of traces of their handiwork on their pictures, from areas of thick impasto to choppy brush strokes of varying lengths to sections of pure, overlapping colors.

By the 1930s, Americans like Louis Betts had lost interest in the attempt to record optical sensations in a scientific way. What remained of Impressionism was the Impressionist style. In the work reproduced here, for example, Betts uses the loose, dashing brush strokes of a Monet or a Renoir to embue his picture with life and energy. The artist combines an opulent display of rich, robust color with a strong dose of homey sentiment. His method is straightforward and honest, and there is great assurance in the emotional mood he creates. Above all, perhaps, the picture is a vigorous expression of American womanhood at its most ideal. Betts poses his pretty young model in a low backed chair, facing right. She is stylishly attired in a fern green dress that sets off her short, fashionable curls. The little girl wears a sunny yellow and white dress and glows with good health. She presses her small body deep into her mother's shoulder, as though seeking shelter from the world's hurts. The emotionalism of this painting—conveyed by the two figures totally absorbed in each other—is enhanced by the rhapsodic lushness of the texture, the rich, glowing colors, and the intimacy of the scene.

By the time she was 15 years old, Marie-Elisabeth-Louise Vigée-Lebrun was earning enough money to support her widowed mother and her younger brother. As a portraitist to Queen Marie Antoinette she had gained a reputation as a born colorist and, as a consequence, became one of the most desired portrait painters in Europe. Then came the bloody French Revolution which forced her to escape from her native land with her young daughter. Crossing the border into Italy one midnight, she spent the next 12 years in exile. During this time she enjoyed a spectacular career, touring the courts of Europe and painting royalty for handsome fees.

Like all of Vigée-Lebrun's portraits, *The Artist and Her Daughter*, painted for her patron d'Angiviller and now in the Louvre, is outrageously flattering. The artist wears the type of high-waisted, classically inspired white shift that she herself helped popularize among a disintegrating aristocratic society. The picture is a masterpiece in which a mother's blind love for her only child shines through in every stroke on the canvas. Lest anyone miss the artist's maternal feelings, Mme. Vigée-Lebrun pictures herself protectively embracing her daughter, who was five or six years old at the time. She later described the girl as ". . . charming in every respect. Her large blue eyes, sparkling with spirit, her slightly tip-tilted nose, her pretty mouth, magnificent teeth, a dazzling fresh complexion—all went to make up one of the sweetest faces to be seen. I saw in my daughter the happiness of my life, the future joy of my old age, and it was therefore not surprising that she gained an ascendancy over me." Predictably, Vigée-Lebrun did not have an easy time with this child, who was considered difficult and spoiled.

*Mother and Child,* c. 1930
LOUIS BETTS, American, 1873–1961
Grand Central Art Galleries, New York City. Oil on canvas.
30 x 25 in.

*The Artist and Her Daughter,* 1789
MARIE-ELISABETH-LOUISE VIGÉE-LEBRUN, French, 1755–1842
The Louvre, Paris. Oil on panel. 51½ x 37 in.

*Portrait of Countess Livia da
Porto Thiene and Her Daughter
Porzia*, 1550s
VERONESE, Italian, 1528–1588
The Walters Art Gallery, Baltimore. Oil on
canvas. 82 x 47⅝ in.

## ♣ *The Protector*

The full-length portrait reproduced here captures Veronese's gentle side as well as the charm of his models. It is an unusually intimate painting in which the artist chooses to emphasize the warm and tender relationship between Countess Livia da Porto Thiene and her daughter Porzia rather than their rank. The countess stands fingering the ornately wrought gold chain that hangs from her waist as her attention is momentarily diverted from her child to someone else, perhaps a servant. She stands alert, her rich ruby brocade dress covered by a spotted fur-trimmed gown that sways slightly on her well-nourished body, her left arm circled protectively around her daughter. Porzia clings to her mother's mantle, her right hand embracing the countess as she bends forward to peer out from behind her flesh-and-blood stronghold.

Mother and child share the same simple hair style, parted down the middle and drawn tightly back against the head. Both wear simple jeweled caps and Porzia's shimmering emerald dress contrasts dramatically with her mother's scarlet frock. The rich apparel gives the painter a chance to display his mastery of lighting effects and his love of expressive coloring. Indeed this opulent portrait allows Veronese to demonstrate the range of his considerable abilities with oil paint. His technical skill coupled with the anecdotal effects that he so lovingly renders reveal his exquisite sensitivity to the individual personalities of his sitters—the countess a glowing picture of perfect poise and refinement and little Porzia struggling hard not to smile as she looks directly out at her audience.

Thus far, art history has recorded the names of only a few African-Americans but it is clear that even at the earliest stages of the nation's cultural development, mainstream American artists were influenced by the pottery and other handicrafts produced by slaves. During the 1920s, the awakening spirit of "Negritude," which encouraged racial pride among African-Americans, fostered a continuing interest in the civilizations of black Africa and redefined the meaning of the black experience in the New World. The result was an era in the arts now called the "Harlem Renaissance," from a neighborhood in Manhattan where a large community of black writers and artists lived and worked.

Among the participants in the black arts revival was Sargent Johnson. His *Forever Free* seen here was first shown in 1935 at the renowned Harmon Foundation exhibition in New York. The piece is of redwood, covered with several coats of gesso and fine linen. Painted black and white and highly polished, it shows a standing mother with her arms close by her sides, her hands protectively covering the figures of the two children who are etched into her blue skirt. The strong bond among the three is evident in the way both children melt into their mother's body. She is a heroic figure, whose vigilant posture and outward glance indicate her determination to protect her children from a hostile world.

Johnson has captured the natural beauty and dignity of the African race in this figure's facial features, hair, bearing, and manner. He also combines modernism and the primitive style that became part of the black aesthetic. It is an astonishing synthesis marked by the elimination of details, the reduction of forms to harmonious, stylized masses, and the use of a rich, copper-brown color in the flesh tones. When this sculpture was first shown critics called it a masterpiece.

*Forever Free,* 1933
SARGENT JOHNSON, American, 1887–1967
San Francisco Museum of Modern Art, Gift of Mrs. E.D. Lederman. Wood with lacquer on cloth. Height 36 in.

# The Enduring

## Bond

*F*lesh of flesh
*Bone of my bone thou art, and from thy state*
*Mine never shall be parted, weal or woe.*


JOHN MILTON
**The Eternal Bond**

**B**ecause the love of children is at the root of family solidarity, and family solidary is in turn a cornerstone of social stability, the maternal instinct became a popular theme among painters rather early on. Angelica Kauffmann's *Cornelia Pointing to Her Children as Her Treasures*, painted in the late 18th century, looks back to Greco-Roman antiquity with a nostalgia for the high-minded human behavior that such civilizations were thought to epitomize. The subject was inspired by the Roman writer Valerius Maximus, who maintained that Cornelia, the daughter of Scipio Africanus and the widow of Tiberius Sempronius Gracchus, was a paragon of modesty and nobility of spirit.

Kauffmann chooses to depict the moment when the widowed Cornelia, who is living on modest means, is visited by a friend of hers, a noblewoman who proudly displays all her beautiful jewels to her unadorned friend. When she asks to see Cornelia's own baubles, the widow gathers about her Tiberius and Gaius, her sons who have just come home from school, and her little daughter, Sempronia, saying "These are my most precious jewels." Heroic Cornelia understood the importance of children, not only for her personally but for the state of Rome. Unlike her selfish friend, she had virtuously sacrificed all of her gems to help fund the noble enterprises of the state. As with her motherly devotion, her willingness to give up her worldly goods for her country was intended to inspire those who viewed this painting. As such, the work reflects the moralizing current that underlay Neoclassical art during the late 18th century.

Produced in Naples for George Bowles, an Englishman who was Kauffmann's most loyal patron, this painting became one of the Swiss artist's best-known works. Highly acclaimed for the subtle modeling of her portraits, the purity of her coloring, and the striking balance of her compositions, she was immensely popular during her lifetime. Indeed, this picture was so well received it was not only engraved, it was even copied in embroidery.

*Cornelia Pointing to Her Children as Her Treasures*, c.1785
ANGELICA KAUFFMANN, Swiss, 1741–1807
Virginia Museum of Fine Arts, Richmond, The Adolph D. and Wilkins C. Williams Fund. Oil on canvas. 40 x 50 in.

# ✢ Grieving

**K**äthe Kollwitz was often labeled the "socialist artist" because of her compassion and pity for her chosen subject, the working-class poor. At the time that she made the print reproduced here she was at work on her famous *Peasant's War* series and was deeply stirred by Black Anna, an elderly woman who was summoning her countrymen to rise against their oppressors. Kollwitz' preparatory drawing for *Mother with Dead Child* reflects Anna's earthy, powerful presence as well as Kollwitz' own. The model for the dead child is the artist's younger son, Peter, then about seven, who posed for the picture across his mother's lap as she gazed into a mirror. The position required great effort. Once, while working, Kollwitz let out a groan, but Peter told her, "Be quiet, Mother, it is going to be very beautiful."

*Woman with Dead Child* shows a sobbing woman hunched over the body of her lifeless offspring. By creating the remarkably powerful, dense passage of black chalk and graphite and adding subtle gold washes, the artist melds the forms into one complex and interlocking organism. This mother and son are inseparable, calling to mind the unique relationship of the Virgin mother and the Christ child. Moreover, Kollwitz' unexpected juxtapositions of the actual and surreal imbue this print with the fantastic quality of nightmare. In trying to capture the full force of emotion that grips the grieving woman, she fills the picture with the strong internal force of her own psyche

This etching serves as an unfailing reminder that, despite the tragic suffering endured by ordinary people, love is the one emotion that can transform human existence and unite all humankind. Kollwitz later called the print prophetic since she ended up surviving both her son and her grandson, also named Peter. The former was killed in World War I, the latter in World War II.

*Woman with Dead Child, 1903*
KÄTHE KOLLWITZ, German, 1867–1945
National Gallery of Art, Washington, D.C., Gift of Philip and Lynn Straus. Engraving and soft-ground etching with black chalk, graphite, and metallic gold paint on heavy-wove paper. 16⅜ x 18⅝ in.

# Leaving the
# Nest

*She gave me childhood's flowers,*
*Heather and wild thyme,*
*Eyebright and tormentil,*
*Lichen's mealy cup*
*Dry on wind-scored stone,*
*The corbies on the rock,*
*The rowan by the burn.*

*Sea-marvels a child beheld*
*Out in the fisherman's boat,*
*Fringed pulsing violet*
*Medusa, sea-gooseberries,*
*Starfish on the sea-floor,*
*Cowries and rainbow-shells*
*From pools on a rocky shore.*

*Gave me her memories,*
*But kept her last treasure:*
*'When I was a lass,' she said,*
*'Sitting among the heather,*
*'Suddenly I saw*
*'That all the moor was alive!*
*'I have told no one before.'*

*That was my mother's tale.*
*Seventy years had gone*
*Since she saw the living skein*
*Of which the world is woven,*
*And having seen, knew all;*
*Through long indifferent years*
*Treasuring the priceless pearl.*

KATHLEEN RAINE
**Heirloom**

*She gave me childhood's flowers,*
*Heather and wild thyme,*
*Eyebright and tormentil,*
*Lichen's mealy cup*
*Dry on wind-scored stone,*
*The corbies on the rock,*
*The rowan by the burn.*

*Sea-marvels a child beheld*
*Out in the fisherman's boat,*
*Fringed pulsing violet*
*Medusa, sea-gooseberries,*
*Starfish on the sea-floor,*
*Cowries and rainbow-shells*
*From pools on a rocky shore.*

*Gave me her memories,*
*But kept her last treasure:*
*'When I was a lass,' she said,*
*'Sitting among the heather,*
*'Suddenly I saw*
*'That all the moor was alive!*
*'I have told no one before.'*

*That was my mother's tale.*
*Seventy years had gone*
*Since she saw the living skein*
*Of which the world is woven,*
*And having seen, knew all;*
*Through long indifferent years*
*Treasuring the priceless pearl.*

KATHLEEN RAINE
**Heirloom**

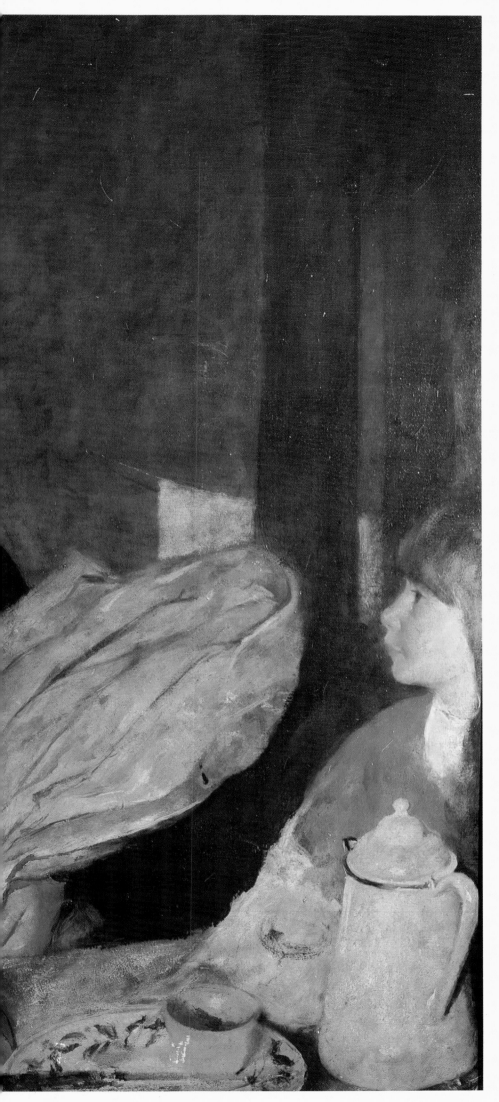

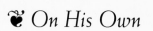

Charles W. Hawthorne was born in Loda, Illinois, but grew up in Richmond, Maine, where his father was a sea captain. Later he moved to Provincetown, Massachusetts, where he founded the Cape Cod School of Art. Attracted to the light, the sea, and the natural beauty of Provincetown, he took as his favorite subject the local Yankee and Portuguese fishermen and their families, whom he depicted with a rare sensitivity.

In *First Voyage* Hawthorne focuses on a traditional subject in art, the breaking of home ties. The scene that he depicts, that of a mother bidding farewell to her son, has been enacted in many Cape Cod homes over the centuries as lads take to the sea in the manner of their fathers before them. To be sure, Hawthorn's painting captures the mood of his sitters—their introspection and the emotional turmoil of the young man who is the center of attention as he readies himself to go out on his own for the first time. Dressed in a black jacket, he stands on the threshold of manhood in all his boyish vulnerability, an overcoat thrown over his right arm. His mother, seated at left, secures a loose button on the worn garment. Her face is full of sadness as she realizes that her chick is leaving the nest. While she no doubt fears what will happen to him as he faces the cruel and uncertain world, she knows that he must go. So she concentrates on getting him ready for his departure while his sisters look passively on.

*First Voyage, 1915*
CHARLES W. HAWTHORNE, American, 1872–1930
Provincetown Art Association and Museum, Massachusetts.
Oil on board. 48 x 60 in. Photo by James Zimmerman.

143

## ❦ A Mother's Dilemma

**B**orn at the turn of the century, Constance Coleman Richardson is a realist painter who uses a classic, 15th-century style learned from museum conservationists. In *Street Light* she applies this age-old technique to the examination of a relatively modern problem, the difficulty that mothers have in separating from their daughters.

Richardson's account is rendered in highly simplified forms and gestures, reminiscent of the work of Edward Hopper and Guy Pene du Bois. It is set on a hot summer night, as a mother and her daughter— seen under the glow of a streetlight—walk together along a suburban street. The child looks up at her mother but the woman ignores the youngster. The realization that her child is entering her teen years and will soon be leaving home for a life of her own is difficult for her to bear. So, instead of finding a way of relating to her growing child, she gazes almost longingly at a younger girl across the street. A man sitting on the steps of his house may be the younger child's father. On a symbolic level, the three female figures may represent childhood, adolescence, and maturity—three stages in a woman's life.

The artist's slice-of-life depiction is compelling because it represents a point faced by every mother, the point when a child stops being a child and crosses the threshold into young adulthood. Like many of her contemporaries, Richardson drew upon her own childhood experiences in her work and, in fact, there does seem to be something autobiographical at play here. This street, these people, look as if they come from memory. But there is also a surrealistic quality to the painting. It almost suggests a dream or a fairy tale, something that flows directly from the unconscious where, as the French writer Hélène Cixous said, "the repressed manage to survive."

*Street Light,* 1930
CONSTANCE COLEMAN RICHARDSON,
American, 1905–
© 1992 Indianapolis Museum of Art, Gift of Mrs. James W. Fesler. Oil on canvas. 28 x 36 in.

Renoir was made a Chevalier of the Legion of Honor. In 1911 he suffered an attack of paralysis which made it difficult for him to paint, although he often worked with the brushes strapped to his hands. He died in 1919 of congestion of the lungs.

**Sir Joshua Reynolds, English, 1723–1792**
Joshua Reynolds was born at Plympton St Maurice in Devon. In 1740, he went to London, where he was apprenticed to the portrait painter Thomas Hudson. Two years later he returned home, started to paint professionally, and from 1743–1749 was in practice on his own in London and Devonshire. In 1749, he journeyed to Rome, where he stayed for two years, becoming proficient at portraiture in the Grand Style. When he returned to England, he was an artistically mature 30-year-old. Seven years later the first public exhibition of his work marked him as the leading portraitist in Britain. He became the first president of the newly founded (1768) Royal Academy and was knighted the following year.

**Constance Coleman Richardson, American, 1905–** Constance Coleman Richardson is a Realist painter who employs classic 15th-century techniques in works that are filled with a deep understanding of the American scene. She attended Vassar College and then spent three years at the Pennsylvania Academy of the Fine Arts. In the 1930s Richardson exhibited widely, painting in a simplified architectonic style reminiscent of that of Edward Hopper and Guy Pene du Bois. Her starkly simplified compositions and suburban scenes capture the quiet and sometimes disquieting features of the American landscape and, although they look as though they faithfully represent actual places, Richardson frequently changes the composition of her locales, as well as alters colors, simplifies forms, and adds figures to establish a desired mood.

**Agnes Millen Richmond, American, 1870–1964**
Agnes Millen Richmond was born in Alton, Illinois, and educated at the St. Louis School of Fine Arts. In 1888 she moved to New York where she studied with John Henry Twachtman, Walter Appleton Clark, and Kenyon Cox at the Art Students League. She later became an instructor at the League. By 1927 she had moved to Brooklyn and was spending her summers in Mountainville, New York. She combined the rural settings of Illinois with the urban life of New York City to create a portfolio of portraits of women from different social backgrounds. The recipient of numerous prizes, including the Watrous Figure Prize in 1911, Richmond exhibited at the Smithsonian Institution, the National Academy of Design, the Carnegie Institute, the Brooklyn Museum, and the Pennsylvania Academy of the Fine Arts.

**Faith Ringgold, American, 1934–** Born and raised in Harlem, New York, Faith Ringgold married a jazz musician, had two daughters, and after a divorce, finished college and taught art in secondary schools. In 1959, while completing a Master's degree at City College of New York under the tutelage of Robert Gwathmey and Yasuo Kuniyoshi, she decided to become a full-time artist. She has since progressed from paintings to three-dimensional works based on African crafts. She is an outspoken feminist and has been instrumental in forming coalitions against racism. Ringgold has repeatedly fought for equality in the arts for men and women regardless of race, creed, sexual orientation, or religion. Her works are in major museum collections in the United States and world-wide.

**Peter Paul Rubens, Flemish, 1577–1640** Peter Paul Rubens was born in Siegen, Westphalia, where his father, an alderman of Antwerp, took up residence after being forced to flee his hometown for practicing Calvinism. From 1600–1608 the young artist lived mostly in Italy, where he obtained important commissions in Genoa and Rome and became court painter to Vincenzo Gonzaga, Duke of Mantua. In 1608 he returned to Antwerp and the following year married Isabella Brant. In 1609 he became the court painter to the Spanish governors of the Netherlands. He was a successful diplomat as well as a painter.

**John Singer Sargent, American, 1856–1925**
Born in Italy of American parents, John Singer Sargent was educated in Italy and France and spent

JOHN SINGER SARGENT: *Portrait of Mrs. Edward L. Davis and Her Son, Livingston Davis*

most of his life abroad. He began his career in Paris, studying with the fashionable portrait painter Charles Carolus-Duran. Adopting the rapid, bravura painting methods of his teacher, Sargent later refined them through an extensive study of the works of Diego Velázquez, Frans Hals, and Édouard Manet. He became a regular exhibitor at the Paris Salons before the scandal surrounding his portrait of Madame X, now in the Metropolitan Museum of Art, which was exhibited in 1884. He was forced to leave Paris for London where he lived thereafter, making occasional visits to the United States. Sargent gained international recognition for his elegant portraits of English aristocrats and American socialites.

**Egon Schiele, Austrian, 1890–1918** At age 15, Egon Schiele, the son of an Austrian stationmaster, entered the Vienna Academy of Arts, where he studied for four years. He first exhibited his work in 1908 at Klosterneuburg, near Vienna. At the end of World War I a decisively successful exhibition of his paintings was arranged by the avant-garde group, the Vienna Sezession. He won critical acclaim for his astonishing draftsmanship and bold, emotionally charged work. He died in the influenza epidemic of 1918, before he reached his full potential as an artist.

**James Jebusa Shannon, Irish, 1862–1923** The son of Irish immigrants, James Jebusa Shannon was born in New York. When he was eight years old, his family moved to Canada, settling in Saint Catharines, Ontario, where he received his first training from a local painter named Wright. On his teacher's advice he continued his studies in London with Sir Edward Poynter. He studied for three years, supporting himself by painting portraits. By the late 1880s Shannon's reputation was established. He was a founding member in 1886 of the New English Art Club and he became a member of the Royal Academy in London in 1897. After 1900 he paid several visits to the United States working mainly in New York. He was elected an associate to the National Academy of Design in 1907.

**Katsukawa Shunshō, Japanese, 1726–1792**
Katsukawa Shunshō was born in Edo and was a pupil of the master Shunsui. Influenced by Hanabuse Itcho, Shunshō was an artist of great ability, one of the first to use the mica print, whose bright metallic surface gave it a hint of preciousness and extravagance. Shunshō must have frequented the *kabuki* theater since he made so many admirable prints of actors. His art was revolutionary in its time. Founder of the Katsukawa school, his pupils included Shunko and Hokusai.

157

**W. Eugene Smith, American, 1918–1978** In 1936/37, Kansas-born W. Eugene Smith attended the University of Notre Dame on a special photography scholarship, where he was influenced by Pulitzer Prize-winning news photographer Frank Noel. In 1937, he joined the staff of *Newsweek* in New York but was fired for not printing his images in the magazine's prescribed format. A year later, he signed with the Black Star agency and began doing freelance photography for *Life, Collier's, Harper's Bazaar,* the *New York Times,* and other periodicals. A year later he joined the staff of *Life,* staying through 1955 and continuing to work for the periodical as a freelancer thereafter. After serving as a war correspondent during the 1940s, Smith taught at the New School of Social Research in New York City and at the School of Visual Arts. Today he is best remembered for his remarkable photo essays in *Life.* He thought of himself as a teacher whose subject was the human condition. Everything he photographed related to his crusade for better human relations.

**Joaquin Sorolla, Spanish, 1863–1923** Joaquin Sorolla was born to humble parents and orphaned at the age of two years. At age 21 he won a scholarship to the Spanish Academy in Rome and from 1890 to 1900 sent paintings to all the leading salons in Madrid, Paris, Munich, Chicago, Berlin, Vienna, and Venice. Sorolla spent most of his working life in Madrid, where he painted monumental works of historical and social value. During the same period he developed his own *plein-air* style, painting landscapes, townscapes, garden scenes, and genre scenes with an extraordinary capacity for capturing light. He was immensely popular during his lifetime and the winner of many awards. Paralyzed by a stroke in 1920, he died in 1923 at 60 years of age. Shortly thereafter his reputation as a painter was submerged in the rising tide of the avant-garde movement and Spain's increasing isolation due to the Civil War.

**Lilly Martin Spencer, American, 1822–1902** Lilly Martin Spencer was born in Exeter, England, but emigrated with her family to New York City in 1830, settling a few years later in Marietta, Ohio. Her considerable artistic talents were quickly recognized and her first public exhibition came in 1841, when she was only 19. In time, she earned a reputation as one of America's important painters of the domestic scene. The mother of 13 children, Spencer, with the aid of her devoted husband, was extremely successful at selling her paintings. The sales of the lithographic reproductions of her canvases also contributed to her widespread popularity. On the day that she died, at age 79, she had spent the morning at her easel.

**Florine Stettheimer, American, 1871–1944** Florine Stettheimer was the second-youngest of four children—three daughters and one son—born to Rosetta Walter and Joseph Stettheimer. Reared in Rochester, New York, she studied art with Kenyon Cox at the Art Students League in Manhattan. Between 1906 and 1914 she traveled abroad with her sisters Ettie and Carrie, studying art in Berlin, Stuttgart, and Munich. They returned to New York at the outbreak of World War I, after which Florine, her mother, and her sisters established a celebrated salon in New York City, entertaining famous artists of the avant-garde.

**Anique Taylor, American** An artist, teacher, poet and clown, Anique Taylor performs for children's shows, is a magician, and writes children's books. Her artistic style is informed by her admiration for Leonardo da Vinci, Michelangelo, Caravaggio, and William Blake. She studied art at Antioch College and has created illustrations for *Artnews* and other publications. A teacher of gifted children, she believes that schooling may inhibit creativity and is actively interested in keeping youngsters in touch with their own inherent expressiveness. "The very things that nurture creativity," she says, "make it hard to teach in the system we've created."

**Abbott H. Thayer, American, 1849–1921** Boston-born Abbott Handerson Thayer grew up in Keene, New Hampshire, and Brooklyn, New York, studying at the Brooklyn Academy of Design and the National Academy of Design. Following his marriage in 1875, he went to Paris where he continued his studies at the École des Beaux-Arts. Returning to the United States in 1879, he joined the newly founded Society of American Artists and opened a studio in Manhattan. Shortly after his wife's death in 1891, he remarried and subsequently began working in Dublin, New Hampshire. During the 1890s and early 1900s, he lived in Italy, where he took on studio assistants for the first time, a practice he continued when he returned to the United States.

**Charleen Touchette, Canadian** Of French-Canadian and Blackfoot Indian descent, Charleen Touchette received a B.A. in painting from Bard College and studied both painting and art history at Wellesley College, Brown University, and the Rhode Island School of Design. She sees balancing the roles of artist and mother as a rewarding challenge. Using her unique worldview and multicultural background, she has created a body of work that examines what it feels like to be a woman, a sister, a daughter, and a mother.

**Utagawa Toyokuni, Japanese, 1769–1825** Utagawa Toyokuni started out as an unpaid painter in the employ of Izumiya Icahibei of the Kansendo publishing house. Before long collectors were clamoring for his polychrome prints and triptychs which commanded substantial prices. He became prosperous and publishers began flocking to him, begging him for work for them. During his lifetime Toyokuni was immensely popular and surrounded by no fewer than 28 pupils. Toyokuni loved sake and buying the favor of geishas. At the age of 40, he married a girl of 15.

**Charles Frederic Ulrich, German-American, 1858–1908** Charles Frederic Ulrich was born in New York of German parents. At the end of the 1870s, after studying at the National Academy of Design, he went to Munich for additional training. It was in Germany that his meticulous attention to detail was developed, along with his ability to render solid, well-drawn forms. There, too, he became particularly interested in genre subjects. He returned to New York in 1883, exhibiting with several groups and receiving considerable recognition for his work. Nevertheless, he eventually returned to Europe, where he married in 1897. He spent the rest of his life abroad traveling about Holland, Germany, and England and was known to be working in Rome around the turn of the century. He died in Berlin in 1908.

W. EUGENE SMITH: *Tomoko and Mother, Minamata, Japan*

**Kitagawa Utamaro, Japanese, 1753–1806** Kitagawa Utamaro is one of Japan's most significant artists. Born in 1753, he lived all his life in the capital city, Edo, a central figure in the culture of the people rather than that of the aristocratic Japanese court. His forms of expression were influenced by *kabuki* plays, light novelettes, comic verse, and earlier color woodcuts. Like other artists of the "Floating World," Utamaro drew his material for the most part from his personal life and from the demi-monde of Edo.

**James Van Der Zee, American, 1886–1983** Born in Lenox, Massachusetts, James Van Der Zee was a self-taught photographer. He obtained his first camera around 1900 and shortly thereafter began a distinguished career that spanned eight decades. During his lifetime Van Der Zee focused his attention primarily on the life and residents of Harlem, compiling in the process an unusual collection of photographs of middle-class black Americans. His portraits include such notables as Bill "Bojangles" Robinson, Joe Louis, Marcus Garvey, and Father Devine. Van Der Zee was awarded an honorary doctorate by Seton Hall University in 1976.

**Veronese (Paolo Caliari), Italian, 1528–1588** Growing up in Verona, Veronese absorbed the traditions of pictorial clarity established by the founders of the Venetian school, Andrea Mantegna and Jacopo Bellini. In 1552 he visited Mantua where he was impressed by the illusionistic style of Mannerist Giulio Romano. A year later he settled in Venice where he won a reputation as a sophisticated decorator. His theatricality, sumptuous coloring, and clever use of perspective brought him patrons and wealth. Nevertheless his ingenious compositions full of striking foreshortening and masterful arrangements of figures sometimes won unwelcome attention. *The Last Supper* (1573, Venice Accdèmia), for example, brought him before the dreaded Inquisition, where he was sharply criticized "for introducing profane elements—dogs, German soldiers, and such things— into a religious picture." Veronese prudently decided to change the title of the picture to *Feast in the House of Levi* and thus escaped criminal charges.

**Marie-Elisabeth-Louise Vigée-Lebrun, French, 1755–1842** Encouraged by her artist-father, the Paris-born Marie-Elisabeth-Louise Vigée-Lebrun pursued her own career as a painter. In 1779 at age 24 she began painting portraits of Marie Antoinette. Over the next decade she won the respect of all of her contemporaries who acclaimed her genius for portraiture. When the French Revolution forced her into 12 years of exile she earned her living by painting royal figures throughout the capitals of Europe. Vigée-Lebrun's courtly manner of painting epitomized the Rococo style. In her

mature years, she adopted a Neoclassical style in which she often portrayed her subjects in simple clothing with a minimum of ornamental detail. Her last years were divided between an apartment in Paris and a summer home in Louveciennes. She died peacefully in Paris at the age of 87.

**Édouard Vuillard, French, 1868–1940** After studying in Paris under the academic painters, William Bouguereau and Jean-Léon Gérôme, Édouard Vuillard fell under the influence of Edgar Degas and Henri Toulouse-Lautrec. In the 1880s he turned away from the dogma of the École des Beaux-Arts and joined the Académie Julian where he was befriended by Pierre Bonnard, Maurice Denis, Paul Sérusier, and Ker-Xavier Roussel. Dissatisfied with the purely visual effects of Impressionism, Vuillard and his friends studied and applied the theories of the Symbolist writers. The Nabis—as the artists called themselves—felt that art should be evocative, expressing a sense of mystery and reflecting the state of the spirit. Vuillard lived with his mother, keeping well away from the art politics of his day and creating most of his paintings in their small family apartment. He was by nature an unusually silent, self-contained person who rarely revealed his private thoughts to others.

**Max Weber, Russian-American, 1881–1961** The son of a poor Jewish tailor in Bialystok, Russia (now Poland), Max Weber emigrated to the United States at age ten, settling in the Williamsburg section of Brooklyn. In the fall of 1905 he traveled to Paris, where he worked under Jean-Paul Laurens at the Académie Julian. While in France he was attracted to the art of several primitive peoples that he saw in museums, including those of Assyria, Egypt, Africa, and archaic Greece. He was also influenced by the work of Paul Cézanne and Henri Matisse. Shortly after his return to the United States in 1909, he became involved in the study of Native American art and the works of their ancestors in Central and South America. From 1914 to 1918 he taught art appreciation at the Clarence White School of Photography in New York and served on and off as an instructor at the Art Students League of New York until around 1927.

**Charles White, American, 1918–1979** Chicago native Charles White taught at the South Side Art Center in the mid-1930s and received a scholarship to the Art Institute of Chicago in 1937. Late in the decade he worked as a muralist for the Works Progress Administration and in 1942 studied painting with Harry Sternberg at the Art Students League in New York. During the 1940s, he became involved with David Siqueiros, Diego Rivera, and other Mexican muralists of the day. His study at the Taller de Gráfica in Mexico City

KITAGAWA UTAMARO: *Woman Grimacing in Mirror at Child on Floor*

in 1947 led him to create graphic works dealing with social themes, centering principally on the struggles of African-Americans and in 1949 he formed the Committee for the Negro in Arts in New York. Traveling to Europe two years later, White achieved an international reputation as a draftsman during the 1950s. In 1969, he cofounded the Black Academy of Arts and Letters and in New York.

**Grace Woodward, American, 1872–1967** In 1905 Grace Woodward was living and working in Rochester, New York, where she was described as one of the city's "most successful photographers." Although she was exposed to the poverty and degradation of the city, she chose to concentrate her talents on portraits, still lifes, and landscapes, always bringing a fresh viewpoint to her work without losing sight of tradition. She was a competent craftswoman, whose career had been shaped by the pictorialist sentiments of the pioneering English photographer, Julia Margaret Cameron. Woodward was a professional photographer and a single, self-supporting woman at a time when most of her peers were devoting themselves to domestic concerns. Today she is remembered for her striking photographs of the women's rights leader Susan B. Anthony.

# Index of Artists and Illustrations